NAVIGATING GRIEF
A Guided Journal

Navigating Grief
A Guided Journal

Prompts and Exercises for
Reflection and Healing

Mia Roldan, LCSW, LCDC

ROCKRIDGE
PRESS

Cover and Interior Designer: Mando Daniel
Art Producer: Meg Baggott
Editor: Samantha Holland
Production Editor: Sigi Nacson
Production Manager: Holly Haydash

Author photo courtesy of Ryan Andrews / @photographeelings

ISBN: Print 978-1-64876-316-8
R0

Dedicated to my dad,
David Lee Knutson, 1931–2021

This journal belongs to:

_____

Contents

Resilience is the process of adapting well in the face of adversity, trauma, tragedy, threats or significant sources of stress. . . . Resilience is not a trait that people either have or do not have. It involves behaviors, thoughts and actions that can be learned and developed in anyone.

—adapted from the American Psychological Association

Introduction

Welcome to your personal place of healing. My name is Mia, and I will be your companion on this journey. I am a wife and the mother of two boys, living with my family in Austin, Texas. I have always worked in the helping professions, first as a special education teacher, and for the last 10 years, as a clinical psychotherapist.

I believe that at the core of all of us are the building blocks for *resiliency*. This is my guiding principle for the therapy work I do, as well as for my own work. This book is a guide to help you process your grief and begin your own journey of resiliency. My goal is to share an authentic description of the different phases of grief and loss, while providing you with compassion and support along the way.

Grief was the soundtrack of my life for many years. My parents had a volatile marriage that lasted much longer than it should have, culminating in the suicide of my mother when I was 12 years old. I spent a lot of time ignoring and denying my pain and felt extremely alone. It wasn't until I found people who understood what I was feeling and who guided me through the darkness that I learned I could do more than just survive. My healing is ongoing, as my grief ebbs and flows. However, I learned over time to transform my grief from defining who I am to instead just being one component of my life's story.

You can find numerous definitions of *grief*, but it's clinically defined as a natural reaction to a significant loss of any kind—not just death. It can also take the form of past regrets, lost opportunities, or remorse for our actions and decisions. None of us are immune to grief, but our experience of it is as unique as we are. Associated emotions can range from a minor interruption of our life to the inability to function, and the frequency and intensity can vary as well. What I know for sure is *there is no right or wrong way to process your grief.* Where you are today in your journey is exactly where you are supposed to be.

Most people are familiar with the "five stages of grief" (denial, anger, bargaining, depression, and acceptance), defined by Swiss psychiatrist Elisabeth Kübler-Ross in her 1969 book, *On Death & Dying*. Clinical professionals now understand that grief is not a linear process, but rather a cycle of emotions that shifts over time and responds to ever-changing circumstances and environments. So, although this book is arranged in five sections to facilitate different reactions to grief and loss, I encourage you to begin where it feels right for you.

Talking about your grief may not be something you've done much, or at all. To encourage the process, this book includes a variety of writing prompts, exercises, affirmations, and quotes. You'll also be invited to practice different kinds of meditation to help refocus and strengthen your mind so that it's easier for you to clear out negative thoughts.

As you look through this book, be open to engaging in whatever calls to you in the moment. Pace yourself through this work, knowing that some days will be more challenging than others. Some days, the words will inspire the healing; other days, the healing will inspire the words. Give yourself permission to start and stop as often as you need. Take your time and know that this book is meant to be a consistent source of hope and inspiration, a means to personal growth.

This book is not a replacement for a therapist, medication, or medical treatment. There is a difference between normal grief and prolonged grief, which is a mental health diagnosis in the *Diagnostic and Statistical Manual of Mental Disorders*, 5th edition (*DSM-5*), called "persistent complex bereavement disorder." There are specific criteria for this disorder that must be "clinically significant" for 12 months or more. If you are experiencing ongoing or debilitating feelings of depression and/or anxiety, I encourage you to consult a medical professional.

We are all on a collective journey of life, and there is much to learn during times of loss. What we're grieving will continue to be a part of who we are, and we can incorporate its essence into our lives with grace and patience. Grief is like a stone thrown into a lake— there is a ripple effect that reaches all aspects of our life. If we do the work and take time to explore our feelings, that energy can be absorbed into a calmness and become a part of us we recognize, but look at with renewed curiosity. In the meantime, be kind to yourself, and know you are not alone.

The Weight of Grief

Any type of loss brings a variety of emotions to the surface, such as denial, anger, guilt, or loss of control. What that looks and feels like is completely unique to you. Initially, we may feel shock and disbelief, and immediately want to retreat to a state of autopilot in order to function in our daily life. We may seek to distance ourself from the reality of the loss to keep intense feelings at bay. Wherever you are, this is your starting point and exactly where you need to be. Now is the time to tend to what your body and mind need in order to nurture your heart. Your willingness to lean into your self-care work throughout the following prompts and exercises will lessen the weight of your grief. Use the quotes and positive affirmations as reminders that you are not alone in your journey, but rather part of a much larger community whose members can relate to your feelings and give you unconditional support and strength.

Core Beliefs

Brainstorm a list of the core values and principles that define you. Write down anything that comes to mind, such as family, loyalty, dependability, honesty, curiosity, civic-mindedness, strength, or compassion. Choose your top three and write them on separate sticky notes. Place these notes on a mirror or somewhere where you'll easily see them. Each week, complete the following sentence and say it out loud: "My intention for the week is to align myself with these three beliefs: _____, _____, and _____."

I am stronger
than I realize and
more powerful
than I know.

Meditation Practice

A different kind of meditation will be included in each section of the book. If you've never meditated, don't worry. The process is simple, and you'll get better at it with practice. When meditating, remember to:

1. Wear comfortable clothing.

2. Silence any electronics and minimize surrounding noises.

3. Choose a quiet space and a comfortable posture, sitting or lying down.

4. Start by spending just a few minutes in meditation, and slowly work up to a longer practice.

We'll begin with a chanting meditation that combines both affirmation and meditation. Every morning, set aside two minutes to practice by focusing your thoughts on the positive affirmation on page 3. Recite or chant the affirmation out loud. Focus on your breath as you exhale these words. Pay attention to the sounds of each individual word. Gradually increase the time as you begin to feel more comfortable. When you finish, check in with yourself. How does your body feel? Where did your mind take you? Record your thoughts here.

_____

_____

_____

_____

_____

Grief can temporarily change how our mind and body work together, and many times people say they just don't feel like themselves. When you feel the weight of your loss, where in your body can you sense it? Do you feel any physical reactions connected to your grief?

_____

_____

_____

_____

_____

_____

_____

_____

_____

_____

_____

_____

_____

When you are grieving, it's helpful to know who you can go to for support. Who in your life comforts you? Write about who they are and how they support you. How do they make you feel when you're with them? Keep this list as a reminder for when you need extra support.

_____

_____

_____

_____

_____

_____

_____

_____

_____

_____

_____

_____

When we focus on gratitude, it brings a sense of positivity and optimism to our daily outlook that can be so healing. Think about all the good things you have right now in your life—all the people and experiences. Create a list of all these elements, big and small, that you're grateful for. Then write about how you can incorporate more gratitude into your life.

_____

_____

_____

_____

_____

_____

_____

_____

_____

_____

_____

Offering Kindness

Self-compassion is essential to our everyday life and even more important when we are grieving. We can easily think of things to say to a friend in pain, but it's more difficult to offer that same kindness to ourselves. Think of how you show compassion to a friend who is suffering. On a small, separate piece of paper (like a notecard), write about how you can offer that same compassion to yourself. Keep it with you as a reminder.

There are people in our life we can talk to anytime, for any reason, and they are a major source of support right now. Below, make a list of people you can talk to about anything. What do you feel comfortable sharing with them? Reach out to one person from your list this week to talk about what kind of support would be helpful right now.

_____

_____

_____

_____

_____

_____

_____

_____

_____

_____

Identify people with whom you have a toxic relationship, as well as activities that only serve as distractions and don't bring you joy. Which ones can you let go of? How can you invite more positivity into your life through supportive connections and activities?

_____

_____

_____

_____

_____

_____

_____

_____

_____

_____

_____

_____

Focusing on self-care is very important when you are grieving. What habits and practices do you have that ground and support you? What other habits could you try to add to your routine? Reflect on these questions, then write about how you can work on this. Include specific actions you can take and a time line to make them happen.

_____

_____

_____

_____

_____

_____

_____

_____

_____

_____

_____

A New Routine

A dependable and consistent routine can help ease the weight of grief. Predictability in our days encourages purpose and decreases anxiety. In the table below, write out your morning and evening routine. Include activities of self-love and self-care, such as reading before bedtime or making a nourishing meal. In a different color pen or pencil, write down a few new ideas you can add to your existing routine.

MORNING ROUTINE	EVENING ROUTINE

Light cannot exist without dark. To deny your own darkness is to deny yourself. To embrace and embody your own shadow will only shift and evolve your relationship with the discomfort of your shadow and the shadow of the collective.

—Sonya Marie Benjamin

What aspects of your life remain solid and strong? What can you count on right now? What goal(s) have you started or are you already working on? What plans for travel or celebrations have you already committed to? Write it all down!

_____

_____

_____

_____

_____

_____

_____

_____

_____

_____

_____

_____

Acknowledging your struggles when you're grieving is a big step toward healing. Think about how your days have been lately. What has been the most difficult part for you? Finish the following sentence in the space below, and write about how it makes you feel.

"The hardest part of the day for me is_____."

_____

_____

_____

_____

_____

_____

_____

_____

_____

_____

_____

_____

Happy Things

Make a list of all the things that bring a smile to your face and make your heart warm. Then create a plan for how you can incorporate one into each day.

- _____
- _____
- _____
- _____
- _____
- _____
- _____
- _____
- _____
- _____
- _____
- _____
- _____

Setting boundaries for yourself when you're grieving is important to protect your mental and physical health. What boundaries do you need to set in order to protect your heart and your body right now? What can you do to put those boundaries in place?

_____

_____

_____

_____

_____

_____

_____

_____

_____

_____

_____

_____

If your loss is due to the death of a loved one, reflect on your memories of them. What is the strongest memory you have of your time with your loved one? Take time to remember and write down as many details as possible—use all your senses to describe the experience.

_____

_____

_____

_____

_____

_____

_____

_____

_____

_____

_____

_____

Your Positive Qualities

Grief can be overwhelming, and sometimes you may feel completely lost. By reminding ourselves of the strengths we possess, we help ground ourselves and orient our view to the present day. For example, are you attentive, loyal, or patient? Write down three affirming positive qualities you see in yourself. Below each one, describe recent occasions when these qualities were demonstrated by your actions.

1. _____

_____

_____

2. _____

_____

_____

3. _____

_____

_____

People instinctively want to be helpful, but often don't know how to express themselves. Asking "How are you doing?" over and over again is not very helpful, and sometimes people make unintentionally awkward statements in an effort to be kind. What has been your experience with this? What are some questions and statements that have helped you? What would be more helpful for people to say to you while you are processing your grief?

_____

_____

_____

_____

_____

_____

_____

_____

_____

_____

_____

Think about a time when you reached out to a grieving friend. What did you say to comfort them? Write those words here. Practice saying these same words of comfort out loud to yourself.

_____

_____

_____

_____

_____

_____

_____

_____

_____

_____

_____

Asking for help improves our resilience by allowing others to instill hope in us, especially in the face of challenging situations. How do you ask for help when you need it? How do you feel accepting this help? How do you think it makes the helper feel?

_____

_____

_____

_____

_____

_____

_____

_____

_____

_____

_____

Your Personal Retreat

Think of a place you've been to in real life or even in your imagination where you feel safe, secure, and at peace. Describe this place using all your senses in the table below. Use this setting as a personal retreat for you to go to when you need it.

SENSES	DESCRIPTIONS
SIGHT	
SOUND	
SMELL	
TASTE	
TOUCH/FEEL	

What activities recharge you and give you energy—mentally and physically? How can you incorporate more of these activities into your week?

_____

_____

_____

_____

_____

_____

_____

_____

_____

_____

_____

When grieving, we may overextend ourselves and make quick decisions without considering all the consequences. In what ways can you give yourself extra space and time every day to make decisions that will honor you and your journey?

_____

_____

_____

_____

_____

_____

_____

_____

_____

_____

_____

It is said that the darkest hour of night came just before the dawn.

—Thomas Fuller

Sit with Your Sadness

The immediate aftermath of a loss centers on the undeniable void left behind—the emptiness that seems to permeate us and even the physical world around us. The void is a stillness and silence that feels impossible to fill with any kind of joy, happiness, or hope. This feeling can turn into a detachment from ourselves and others. Yet it is in this phase that true friendship, kindness, and generosity of spirit come to the surface. For as impenetrable as our sadness feels, it is not a permanent state, but rather an opportunity to nurture our mind, body, and soul. Hope and resiliency are strengthened in darkness. Let the quiet of this moment allow you to open yourself to the light that comes from unexpected people, places, and experiences.

Create your own affirmation about happiness and write it down below. Throughout the week, write about your reasons for why you deserve to be happy in the space provided. Choose one or two to write on sticky notes, and then place them where you can see them often.

_____

_____

_____

_____

_____

_____

_____

_____

_____

_____

_____

I am
stronger
than any
storm.

The process of spiritual meditation incorporates silence and self-control to build a deeper connection to our sources of strength. Think about the affirmation on page 33, and reflect on other times that an event came into your life like a storm. What happened? What lessons did it teach you? What new life tools, such as strengths or lessons, did you gain that you could tap into now?

_____

_____

_____

_____

_____

_____

_____

_____

_____

_____

_____

Let's concentrate on being truly grounded in the here and now. What are expectations you have for yourself today? Now dig more deeply: Which ones are focused on self-care? How can you meet *those* expectations today?

_____

_____

_____

_____

_____

_____

_____

_____

_____

_____

_____

_____

Rising with the Sun

Set an intention to watch the sun come up one morning this week. This can be done outside, or from a window, whatever works best for you. Wake up beforehand with enough time to get a hot beverage for yourself and put on some comfortable clothing. While you're watching the sun slowly rise, repeat an affirmation to yourself. Afterward, reflect. How did spending this time make you feel? Write down your thoughts in the space below.

_____

_____

_____

_____

_____

_____

_____

_____

_____

_____

_____

What words of comfort and healing do you want others to say to you right now? List at least five statements in the space provided, and then say them out loud to yourself. How do you feel after hearing those statements?

_____

_____

_____

_____

_____

_____

_____

_____

_____

_____

_____

_____

If your best friend experienced a loss, what would you say to them? What expectations would you have of them? What would you want to show them? Now, reflect on what you wrote. Would any of these words be helpful for you to hear?

_____

_____

_____

_____

_____

_____

_____

_____

_____

_____

_____

_____

Loving Acceptance

Allowing yourself to accept and hold the feelings that arise is so essential to your journey. Find a quiet and private space to sit, and allow all your feelings to come to the surface. Invite them in, without judgment, and be curious about each one. Come back to this exercise when you begin to feel overwhelmed by your grief. If this exercise feels overwhelming, or you're not ready for this kind of introspection just yet, give yourself permission to stop. It's okay to take a break and sit with those feelings, too.

Follow up on the previous exercise. by completing the sentence below. Allow yourself to honor and recognize the importance of all your feelings. Come back to this practice each day and complete it over the next week in the space provided.

"I give myself permission to _____."

_____

_____

_____

_____

_____

_____

_____

_____

_____

_____

Natural Release

This exercise allows you to name the emotions coming up for you right now, recognize them, and then let them go to demonstrate that you are in control of your feelings. Go outside and collect 10 leaves large enough to write on. With a pen or marker, complete this sentence on each one: "I am releasing _____." Find a nearby stream or body of water. Place each leaf in the water after reading it aloud.

Even if joy feels far off, let's connect with your idea of joy as a counterbalance to what you may be experiencing. What are at least three things that make you feel happy and fulfilled? List what they are and describe why they make you feel this way. If this feels too overwhelming, begin with one for today. Revisit this prompt again when you feel ready.

_____

_____

_____

_____

_____

_____

_____

_____

_____

_____

_____

_____

Reflect on what sadness means to you. Write down all the words and phrases that you immediately associate with the word *sadness*. Then look back over what you wrote. What does this list tell you about your experience with sadness? Can you find any connections to your present-day sadness?

_____

_____

_____

_____

_____

_____

_____

_____

_____

_____

_____

Your Healing Soundtrack

Music is a powerful form of healing, and it can often express our feelings better than we can in words. Create a playlist of songs that have motivated and inspired your spirit in difficult times. Set time aside to listen to your playlist now, and whenever you need some inspiration.

What events, memories, and/or people trigger sadness related to your loss? This is important to be aware of so that you can prepare coping strategies in advance. Write about those triggers here, and create strategies for each one that will help comfort you in those moments.

_____

_____

_____

_____

_____

_____

_____

_____

_____

_____

_____

_____

Tears are the soup of sorrow. The more tears you shed, the more they will wash away your grief. Eventually you'll be able to forget what caused you so much pain.
—Nahoko Uehashi

Mindful Silence

Take a 30-minute mindful walk outside, either early in the morning or late in the afternoon. If walking is not an option for you, find a quiet place outside to sit privately. Leave your phone, or any other distraction, at home, if you can. Use your senses to experience everything you encounter. Take full breaths in through your nose and long exhales out through your mouth for as long as is comfortable (or what you have time for). Set an intention to carry this experience of quiet with you in your day.

One aspect of healing can be achieved by sharing thoughts that you didn't ever get a chance to say. In the space below, write a letter to your loved one or to what you've lost. Recognize what they meant to you, the lessons or ideas you learned from them, and how they will continue to contribute to your life.

_____

_____

_____

_____

_____

_____

_____

_____

_____

_____

_____

_____

A Healing Light

Let's make a Memory Lantern! This is a simple and creative way to connect to your loss through art; specifically, a light to symbolize the lasting connection that will always exist between you and your loss. All materials should be available at your local craft store or online.

Materials

- ☐ Tissue paper
- ☐ Markers
- ☐ Foam Brush
- ☐ Glue or Mod Podge
- ☐ Glass jar
- ☐ LED or votive candle

Directions

1. Cut small squares of tissue paper large enough to write on.

2. On the squares of tissue paper, draw or write about your favorite memories of whom or about that which you are grieving.

3. Use the foam brush to spread the glue or Mod Podge on the back of the squares, attaching the squares onto the outside of the jar.

4. Once the jar has dried, place an LED candle inside your lantern. Move your lantern to an area where you can reflect quietly.

5. If you're so inclined, say a blessing or an affirmation as you light the candle.

Self-care is always important, but especially when we're grieving. Our needs can get lost or forgotten during this phase of immense sadness. How do *you* define self-care? How do you practice self-care regularly? Is there a self-care practice you want to try? What ideas can you add to your self-care list, and how can you integrate them into your daily life?

_____

_____

_____

_____

_____

_____

_____

_____

_____

_____

_____

_____

_____

_____

_____

_____

_____

_____

_____

_____

_____

_____

_____

_____

_____

The stories we have about what we've lost—whatever it may be—can instantly connect us to the spirit of that entity. Share a personal memory about a meaningful experience with whom or what you've lost in the space below.

_____

_____

_____

_____

_____

_____

_____

_____

_____

_____

_____

_____

_____

Food is often tied to strong memories of people, places, and life events. Find a recipe that comforts you. Plan to make it and then share it with others. Afterward, reflect on these questions: How does this food nourish you physically and emotionally? How did the experience of making and sharing your food with others feel? Share that story here.

_____

_____

_____

_____

_____

_____

_____

_____

_____

_____

_____

Disconnect to Reconnect

How are you showing self-care with social media? Do you follow people and pages that are healing for you right now? What about other forms of media consumption such as TV, movies, newspapers, or blogs? Revisit what media you engage with and monitor how much time you're spending on these platforms. Try limiting your media consumption for a day and see how you feel. Use some of this free time to take a 30-minute mindful walk (or sit) outside. Leave your phone at home, if you can. Use your senses to thoroughly experience everything you encounter. Take full breaths in through your nose and long exhales out through your mouth. Set an intention to carry this experience of quiet with you throughout your day.

Write about someone in your life you are grateful for. Maybe it's a close friend or neighbor, or the friendly checkout clerk at your grocery store. What impact have they had on your life? What do you admire about them? What would you like to tell them?

_____

_____

_____

_____

_____

_____

_____

_____

_____

_____

_____

Describe a time when you've helped someone when they really needed it. How do you think it made them feel? What was the experience like for you? How can you show that same kindness to yourself right now?

_____

_____

_____

_____

_____

_____

_____

_____

_____

_____

_____

_____

Taking care is one way to show your love.
Another way is letting people take good
care of you when you need it.

—Fred Rogers

Make Room for Difficult Emotions

Once some time has passed, and your loss has begun to shift to a reality, different emotions may come to the surface. There is no way to know what you will experience. Your grieving process will depend on variables such as how you cope with particular situations, your previous experiences with grief, and the circumstances of your situation. When grieving the loss of a loved one, for example, a variable might be what your relationship was like with that person, or the circumstances surrounding their death. I encourage you to confront and name your feelings as they come, whatever the intensity or frequency. Remember, grief is a natural reaction to any loss, and there is no timetable or manual to tell us what to expect. Prioritizing your mental and physical health is essential right now. The following prompts and exercises will help you identify, express, and make sense of your emotions.

What does true happiness look like for you? When have you experienced it in the past? Take some time to think about these questions. Then complete this sentence:

"I am worthy of happiness because _____."

_____

_____

_____

_____

_____

_____

_____

_____

_____

_____

_____

I understand that self-healing takes time, and I give myself permission to show up fully, each day of the journey, no matter how long it takes.

Mindful Meditation

A consistent meditation practice can transform your experience and perspective. In the stillness comes a calm that no one can take from you. This peace will allow you to remember what you've lost from a new perspective of what it meant to you in the moment, and the meaning you will continue to carry with you. Here we'll practice a mindfulness meditation, which is about cultivating understanding and self-knowledge. Find a quiet space inside or outside to sit comfortably for 10 to 15 minutes. Focus on the affirmation on page 63, repeating it to yourself. Breathe in deeply through your nose and exhale slowly through your mouth. Come back to this exercise anytime you need a minute of mindfulness.

The state of mindfulness can be compared to a "You are here" circle on a map. We are grounded when we are in the here and now. Complete the sentence below. What are some other ways you can ground yourself throughout the week? Write down your answers in the lines provided.

"Today I will focus on _____."

_____

_____

_____

_____

_____

_____

_____

_____

_____

_____

Motivation can be a challenge when grieving a loss. The lack of energy can affect our sleep and make it hard to remember to eat, do laundry, go grocery shopping, or complete other daily tasks. Write out what you need to take care of this week. What are at least three questions to ask yourself every morning to generate motivation for self-care?

_____

_____

_____

_____

_____

_____

_____

_____

_____

_____

_____

Warm Feelings

Make yourself a cup of herbal tea. As the kettle heats, breathe in deeply through your nose and exhale slowly through your mouth. Keep your focus on the activity and notice your feelings. Come back to this exercise anytime you need a break.

What big emotions showed up for you today? What did you do with them? How did you show patience and self-compassion? If you didn't, that's okay, too. Write about how you can show yourself compassion next time a big emotion arises.

_____

_____

_____

_____

_____

_____

_____

_____

_____

_____

_____

_____

One big emotion associated with grief is guilt. Sometimes it's from actions not taken or things not said. Guilt can even come from temporarily forgetting the loss and enjoying a moment. Anger toward ourselves can then fuel these thoughts, and we take it out on ourselves further. Think of at least five ways you can be kind to yourself and write them down. Circle the one that stands out to you most and commit to doing that for yourself this week.

_____

_____

_____

_____

_____

_____

_____

_____

_____

_____

Cost-Benefit Analysis

Worry and fear are companions of grief, but remember: *You are always in control of how you feel and how you respond.* Write down your fears in the space provided and, for each one, list the advantages and disadvantages of holding on to them versus the advantages and disadvantages of letting them go.

HOLDING ON TO FEARS	
ADVANTAGES (BENEFITS AND REWARDS)	DISADVANTAGES (COSTS AND RISKS)

LETTING FEARS GO	
ADVANTAGES (BENEFITS AND REWARDS)	DISADVANTAGES (COSTS AND RISKS)

Out of suffering have emerged the strongest souls; the most massive characters are seared with scars.

—Khalil Gibran

Feeling grounded and settled is both a mental and a physical state. When grieving, it may be difficult to recall what can make you feel better. Write down as many answers as you can to this sentence: "I feel at ease when . . . " Refer back to these answers when you need a reminder.

_____

_____

_____

_____

_____

_____

_____

_____

_____

_____

Grief brings so many questions, from existential ones about the meaning of life to functional ones like "How will I be able to go back to my regular routine?" Answers aren't easy to come by, and sometimes there are none. This creates doubt and uncertainty, which can become a never-ending cycle. Think about where you are right now from the perspective of a younger, more trusting version of yourself. What advice would a younger you offer about your loss? Shifting perspectives helps us view problems in a new light, and our younger selves can remind us of the power of trust, faith, and belief that still exists beneath the surface.

Creating Boundaries

It is always a courageous act to show self-love and self-compassion. Too often, we overextend ourselves, work long hours, skip a meal, or get too little sleep. When shouldering the weight of grief, we can make even more demands on ourselves. Where can you feel yourself overdoing? Where do you need some boundaries in your life? How can you shift that energy toward yourself, your rest, and your well-being? Make a plan in the space below for self-care and setting boundaries.

_____

_____

_____

_____

_____

_____

_____

_____

_____

_____

For a little while, unplug from all media outlets. Slow your pace so that you can connect with people and projects. Allow for mindful contemplation and sharing. How can you give yourself this time every day? Can you designate some defined times during the day to go on your social media or check emails? Can you make a list of people you would like to connect with this during free time? How about projects you'd like to begin? What does mindful contemplation look like for you?

_____

_____

_____

_____

_____

_____

_____

_____

_____

_____

_____

Feeling overwhelmed is a normal part of grief. We constantly place expectations on ourselves in many areas of our life. In order to restore balance, go back to your values from page 2 and consider what is causing them the most stress or strain. Are there things you can reschedule, cancel, or ask someone else to do? Do you need to put some boundaries in place, such as telling others no, changing your mind about a prior commitment, or taking a break from an activity?

_____

_____

_____

_____

_____

_____

_____

_____

_____

_____

_____

_____

Honor Your Anger

When feelings of anger arise, take the time to write them out exactly as they come to you. No matter who or what your anger is directed at, know that it's okay to be mad. Release your feelings on a separate piece of paper and read each statement out loud. When you're finished, tear up the paper. This process—writing, reading, tearing— will aid you in recognizing, validating, and then releasing your anger.

Sometimes short, inspirational phrases can be just the motivation you need in the moment. Maybe you have a favorite affirmation or read one recently that resonates with you. In the space below, write about some that you've come across. Then create your own affirmation for when you're feeling overwhelmed by grief. Write it here and on a sticky note. Place the note where you'll see it often. Reflect on it daily. What does this affirmation do for you? Change the affirmation as you wish or as your feelings change.

_____

_____

_____

_____

_____

_____

_____

_____

_____

_____

Overwhelming grief can cause stress to build up in our body and our mind. Pause and think about the concept of *relief*. What does relief look like for you? How does it feel? Share your recent experiences of relief here.

_____

_____

_____

_____

_____

_____

_____

_____

_____

_____

_____

Exercise and movement greatly reduce stress. Anything that gets you moving is beneficial, such as dancing, walking, yoga, even simple stretches. Take this at your own pace and do whatever activity is available and practical for you. How can you incorporate more movement into your daily routine?

_____

_____

_____

_____

_____

_____

_____

_____

_____

_____

There is power and healing in kindness, which is why we have a Random Acts of Kindness Day, established in 1995. There are many ways to express and receive kindness from others. Write about the last time someone was unexpectedly kind to you. What impact did it have on you?

_____

_____

_____

_____

_____

_____

_____

_____

_____

_____

_____

Your Healing Place

Many reminders of your loss can trigger grief. It may feel overwhelming at times. If you're grieving the loss of a loved one or your grief is due to losing something else that was important to you, create a special place for remembering your loss. Maybe it's a park near your home, a private spot in your backyard, or a comfortable chair in your house. Set an intention to use this space when you want to sit with your memories.

Let's put the focus on your well-being. What activities make you feel relaxed and gratified? Make a list and circle two or three to do this weekend. How do you feel after engaging in one of these relaxing acts?

_____

_____

_____

_____

_____

_____

_____

_____

_____

_____

_____

_____

Dreams are a way our subconscious processes events and emotions. Dreams often reflect our fears and wishes. Share a dream you've had about your loss in the space provided. What happened? If you're grieving the loss of a loved one, experience the dream from their perspective and imagine how they would react. What new observations can you take away?

_____

_____

_____

_____

_____

_____

_____

_____

_____

_____

_____

Healing Connections

In the beginning, our grief seems to be connected to certain places and/or events around us. If your grief is due to the death of a loved one or the loss of an important relationship, pick an interest related to your loved one or your loss, then choose an activity to experience or participate in that is connected to that interest—but only when you are ready. Maybe it's a sporting event, a movie, a concert, or karaoke. Reflect on how this experience connects you to your loved one or your loss.

For us all to remember: Listen to your heart and trust the direction you are being pulled. Something inside you already knows what to do.

—Spring Washam

Take Comfort in Not Having All the Answers

You may be returning to familiar activities, more everyday interactions with others, or various aspects of your regular routine. Some situations may immediately connect you back to your loss, such as driving past a restaurant where you frequently ate with your loved one or seeing a pregnant woman after your miscarriage. Whatever the situation, it's very disorienting to be faced with such a major life transition, and you may feel overwhelmed by all the unanswered as well as *unanswerable* questions, such as "Why did this happen?" or "What if I had [blank]?" I know how challenging and painful this stage can be. Know that you are exactly where you need to be right now—your grief is evidence of your care and love. With the following journal exercises and prompts, I invite you to sit with all the unknowns, and allow for the ebb and flow of your grief to forge a new definition of your existence without what was lost.

In moments of intense emotion, such as pain and sadness, we can feel a connection to something greater than ourselves. There are many ways to define this uniquely personal concept, but I'll use the term *spirituality*. Write about a time you felt connected spiritually to an energy or power outside of yourself. How did it feel? What were your takeaways from the experience? Is there something from that time that applies to this moment?

_____

_____

_____

_____

_____

_____

_____

_____

_____

_____

_____

_____

Breathe.
I am safe.
I am here.
I am resilient.

Sensory Meditation

Let's practice focused meditation. The purpose is to quiet your mind and suspend thoughts about all of those questions surrounding your loss. Go outside and choose an item, such as a bench or a tree, and set an intention to focus your undivided attention on this object. Notice all the shapes, lines, colors, shading, textures, and surfaces. Breathe in deeply through your nose and exhale slowly through your mouth. Sustain your focus for 10 minutes, or however long feels comfortable, and then observe how your mind and body feel when you're finished.

A linking object is a keepsake that binds you to what is gone. It represents the enduring connection you will always have to your loss. Mine is a heart-shaped paper-weight my mom gave me for Valentine's Day. Your linking object can be anything you've kept that has a story connected to your loss. The item can help you sit with the sadness you feel, while also allowing you to move onward in your life without what you've lost. Find your linking object, and write about what it feels like to hold it and what meaning it has for you.

_____

_____

_____

_____

_____

_____

_____

_____

_____

_____

To ground yourself in positivity right now, think about a person who has had a particularly constructive influence on you. Maybe it's a mentor, a teacher, or a neighbor. Write the story of this person and the impact they've had on your life.

_____

_____

_____

_____

_____

_____

_____

_____

_____

_____

_____

_____

Loving Affirmations

Make an affirmation jar. Find any size jar and cut strips of paper. Write 10 to 20 affirming notes to yourself, similar to the affirmation on page 93. Think of this as writing a love letter to yourself. Read your affirmations daily to remind yourself of your value, self-compassion, and strength during this time of uncertainty.

Everything exists in a continuous cycle. From lunar phases to the life cycle to the four seasons of nature, cycles allow us to live more fully in the moment while appreciating change and the layers of ourselves, our relationships, and the world around us. Cycles also provide consistency and predictability that can especially help with grounding. How does your loss allow you to show up as you are right now, instead of feeling that you need to think or act in a certain way?

_____

_____

_____

_____

_____

_____

_____

_____

_____

_____

*The dealing with grief cannot be bypassed.
It is a road you must walk, a race you must
finish and no one else can do it for you.*

—Kate McGahan

Think of people you know, or know of, whom you admire. This can be anyone—celebrities, acquaintances, philanthropists, artists, friends, or musicians. What characteristics in them do you respect? Write about how you see these qualities in yourself, and the steps you can take to cultivate more of these traits.

_____

_____

_____

_____

_____

_____

_____

_____

_____

_____

It can be really difficult to recognize our own growth and resilience. Think of something you can do today that you couldn't a year ago. Or think of a way you have changed something important about yourself in the last year. Share your story here.

_____

_____

_____

_____

_____

_____

_____

_____

_____

_____

_____

_____

_____

Let It Go

This exercise is meant to be a literal and metaphorical release of your grief, as well as a way to bring some levity to your day. Pick up a bottle of bubbles next time you are out. Now go somewhere outside where you have space and privacy. As you blow the bubbles, verbalize what you are releasing and allow it to disappear as the bubbles pop.

Vulnerability is a state of emotional uncertainty that makes us feel that taking action is too risky. However, when we face that fear, we find our true courage and discover an opportunity for growth and change. When have you felt most vulnerable? Did you embrace or resist the experience? Are there any parallels to your present situation? How can you face any fears going forward?

_____

_____

_____

_____

_____

_____

_____

_____

_____

_____

_____

_____

Release the Guilt

This ritual will help you release your thoughts about guilt connected to your loss. You may need to repeat it several times; that's okay. First, write out your feelings of guilt on pieces of scrap paper. What guilt have you been holding on to? Next, use a fireplace, firepit, or candle to burn each thought. Make sure you have a bucket of water or a sink nearby, just in case. You can also tear each one up and place it into a trash can or recycle bin, if that feels safer to you. Say your feelings aloud as you release each individual thought.

After the ritual on the facing page, write down statements that illustrate self-forgiveness and self-compassion to offset any feelings of guilt connected to your loss. Read them back to yourself. Do any of them speak to your heart more than others? If so, write those down on a sticky note and place them where you will see them often.

_____

_____

_____

_____

_____

_____

_____

_____

_____

_____

_____

_____

A Day Just for You

Even when we take a day off, we load it with errands and chores. Create a day that's all about you, and make a plan for it in the space below. Focus on yourself, your needs, and your self-care. Give yourself permission to have a whole day off from obligations. Plan your ideal day from start to finish. Will you sleep in or wake up to watch the sun rise? Watch a movie at home or go out to a movie, read a book, or take a walk in the park? Have dinner at a favorite place or make a special recipe? Whatever you want to do, the day is yours.

Think back to a time when you were really motivated to pursue something (a personal goal, a hobby, a degree in school, or a job). What was your process for maintaining self-discipline? What kept you inspired to continue? How can you apply that determination to what you're experiencing now?

List the top three values that define who you are—such as honesty, loyalty, perseverance, working hard, or being compassionate. Refer to page 2 if you need to. Describe a time when these principles allowed you to help others. How did you feel after the experience?

_____

_____

_____

_____

_____

_____

_____

_____

_____

_____

_____

_____

Reconnect
Through Touch

The internet and social media have created a new way for individuals and groups to connect and communicate. Some have grown used to this new virtual way of socializing, and it has allowed many of us to connect in situations where in-person interactions weren't possible. However, physical distance between family and friends, and what feels like a reliance on technology, can complicate connections, especially in times of grief. Therapeutic touch activates and produces a sense of calm and safety. Reconnect to that physical touch and place a hand (or both hands) on parts of your body while simultaneously taking several deep breaths. You can also gently rub or stroke your heart, shoulders, abdomen, arms, thighs, or face, if that feels comfortable for you.

Forgiveness, Part 1: Who is someone you need to forgive connected to your loss? How has a lack of forgiveness caused you pain? Forgiveness is about the actions of a person, not their character. Write down the events of the wrongdoing. At the end, write and then say aloud, "I forgive [name] for [offense]."

_____

_____

_____

_____

_____

_____

_____

_____

_____

_____

_____

Forgiveness, Part 2: While practicing forgiveness, we often realize that we need to forgive ourselves, too. In retelling any wrongdoing connected to the loss, are there elements you feel responsible for? What additional suffering has this caused? Share your responsibility here. At the end, write and say aloud, "I forgive myself for [offense]."

_____

_____

_____

_____

_____

_____

_____

_____

_____

_____

_____

_____

_____

Loving Exercise

This exercise is simple and straightforward but also incredibly powerful. I invite you to have patience and grace with yourself. Stand in front of a mirror and say, "I love you" to yourself 100 times. If you cannot get to 100, that's okay. Take a break and try again. With practice you will get there. Try to do this every day for a week. What was this experience like for you each day, and as time went on?

When do you feel most connected to your loss? Do certain objects or people trigger your sense of loss? Reflect on these questions to bring a larger awareness to how often and when your thoughts are focused on the loss.

_____

_____

_____

_____

_____

_____

_____

_____

_____

_____

_____

_____

Reflect on what you wrote on page 115. In what ways can you begin to protect yourself from the connections to your loss that evoke pain? How can you begin to advocate for what you need right now? Write about the things you can do to provide for your mental self-care. Be as detailed and thorough as possible.

_____

_____

_____

_____

_____

_____

_____

_____

_____

_____

_____

How do you define *unconditional love*? What would you do differently if you loved yourself unconditionally? Write down your ideas and then circle three items from your list that you can begin to incorporate into your daily life. Write about the difference these actions make.

_____

_____

_____

_____

_____

_____

_____

_____

_____

_____

_____

_____

To be lost is as legitimate a part of your process as being found.

—Alex Ebert

We Grieve in Order to Find Peace

Our journey through grief is about adapting and finding harmony in different realms of our lives. We are compelled to make some concrete change, in deep and less tangible ways. The goal here is to recognize that *you* are creating your own road map of your healing. We search for validation and answers from others, but ultimately the journey is ours to define. The tasks of grieving will become part of all the other recurring self-care tasks you perform daily. Healing is not linear, but rather reflects how much you are willing to show up as an active participant in your consistent self-care and well-being. Doing so creates a new awareness of the world around you and the opportunities for healing that exist. With this awareness also comes clarity—of your direction, your role, and how you want to show up for yourself and others. This last set of prompts and exercises will help you reflect on the many lessons to be discovered in your grief and beyond.

We often lose sight of our adaptability when we are grieving. Take some time to reflect: Over the last few weeks, how have you adjusted to a new normal? Have you gone outside your comfort zone to any degree? What did those moments feel like?

_____

_____

_____

_____

_____

_____

_____

_____

_____

_____

_____

_____

_____

My hopes,
not my hurts,
shape my future.

What has your loss taught you about growth, balance, and purpose? How can these lessons be part of your outlook now and continue to teach you?

_____

_____

_____

_____

_____

_____

_____

_____

_____

_____

_____

Loving Kindness For All

Let's practice a loving-kindness meditation. The aim is to instill a deeper sense of self-worth, empathy, and gratitude through a repetition of kind words, initially directed toward you and then to others. Find your quiet space and repeat phrases aloud such as "May you be happy," "May you find peace," etc. Continue this for several days until you are ready to direct this love and kindness intentionally to others by saying out loud, "May [insert name] be happy."

As you reach the end of this book, how do you see your life being different now as a result of the work you've done? In what ways has it stayed the same?

_____

_____

_____

_____

_____

_____

_____

_____

_____

_____

_____

_____

Your Grief Community

So much healing can happen in a group setting. Being with others who understand exactly what you're going through is invaluable. Find and consider joining a grief and loss support group in your community. Often, there is no fee to join. Or start a group of your own. Gather those you know who have experienced any kind of loss and create a space in your home to share stories, hold each other's pain, and be heard. Check out the Resources (page 151) for more information and to find support groups.

If you're mourning the loss of someone you had a difficult relationship with, what would you want to tell them now? Write a letter to them that shares everything you'd want them to know.

_____

_____

_____

_____

_____

_____

_____

_____

_____

_____

_____

Celebrating Life

If your loss is due to the death of a loved one, try hosting a potluck dinner to celebrate their life. Plan for your loved one to be the guest of honor. Invite others connected to this person. Ask everyone to bring a dish that reminds them of the person. Share stories, photos, and memories. Encourage others to bring stories and photos, as well. You can also host this event virtually in order to include those who live far away.

When grieving your loss, it's comforting to remember all the ways you are still connected. It can be what you shared, or a more subtle quality, such as a value instilled in you from the experience or the relationship. Reflect here on how you feel most connected to your loved one or loss.

_____

_____

_____

_____

_____

_____

_____

_____

_____

_____

_____

You may not control all the events that happen to you, but you can decide not to be reduced by them.

—Maya Angelou

With the transformative change that a loss will bring, we often experience a shift in our priorities. Reflect on how this statement resonates with you. What has become more important? What has become less so?

_____

_____

_____

_____

_____

_____

_____

_____

_____

_____

_____

_____

Your Inspirations

Create an inspiration board. Similar to a vision board, this is a collection of images, phrases, and words that evoke joy, hope, and thoughts of your future.

Materials

- ☐ Poster board (optional)
- ☐ Scissors
- ☐ Glue stick
- ☐ Magazines

Directions

1. Use the space on the facing page to plan out your board. Then create it on a piece of poster board, or use the facing page for your board. This is all about you and just for you.

2. Cut and glue pictures, phrases, and words on the paper.

3. Indulge in your artistic side and add any embellishments you'd like.

4. Place your inspiration board somewhere where you will see it often, as a reminder of what inspires you.

Past regrets are meant to be learned from, not used as a means of self-punishment. They remind us of where we've been, but they don't have to dictate where we're going. Write down any regrets you have about your loss and the lessons you've learned from it.

As you've journaled and reflected on your loss throughout this book, what permissions have you given yourself during difficult times? What were the circumstances that called for each act of permission? How do you plan on giving yourself this grace as you continue your healing journey?

_____

_____

_____

_____

_____

_____

_____

_____

_____

_____

_____

Get It Done

Below, list five tasks or errands you've had sitting on your "to-do" list for some time. Block out time in your week to accomplish them. Reflect here how you felt after you checked these tasks off your list.

1. _____

2. _____

3. _____

4. _____

5. _____

_____

_____

_____

_____

_____

Allowing ourselves to believe and accept that we deserve unconditional love requires commitment and practice. What experiences have taught you to offer yourself grace so far in this journey? How can you continue practicing unconditional love toward yourself? Which practices have helped the most?

_____

_____

_____

_____

_____

_____

_____

_____

_____

_____

_____

What new boundaries have you set for yourself that serve to protect your healing process? Are there more you can set? If so, how will they serve you?

_____

_____

_____

_____

_____

_____

_____

_____

_____

_____

_____

Any act of courage—small or large—inspires us as individuals and as a society. Facing our fears and doing what is right are often contagious and provide the motivation we all need sometimes. Brainstorm courageous acts and courageous people that have influenced you. What lessons can you take away that will help you on your grief journey?

_____

_____

_____

_____

_____

_____

_____

_____

_____

_____

_____

_____

_____

Sending Gratitude

Think of at least three people in your life who you are grateful for. These could be family or friends, people you haven't talked to in a while, coworkers, college roommates, or neighbors. Write each of them a thank-you letter sharing your gratitude. Then mail your letters!

What habits do you have that cause you to compare yourself to others? How can you let go of those judgmental practices?

_____

_____

_____

_____

_____

_____

_____

_____

_____

_____

_____

_____

It's easy to love certain qualities about ourselves, and difficult to love other aspects. But you don't need to love everything about yourself to cultivate self-love. All you need to do is accept what you cannot love. Make a list of aspects of yourself you're not ready to love but you're willing to accept. After completing the following statements of acceptance, reflect on how you feel.

- I accept _____

- I accept _____

- I accept _____

- I accept _____

- I accept _____

- I accept _____

_____

_____

_____

_____

_____

_____

If you're mourning the loss of someone you loved, think about any experiences in which you've communicated with them since their death, either by dreaming about them, sensing their presence, or experiencing other unexplained coincidences. If your loss was something else, reflect on how it has come up for you in dreams or other experiences. Are these experiences comforting or distressing, or both?

_____

_____

_____

_____

_____

_____

_____

_____

_____

_____

_____

What we once enjoyed and deeply loved we can never lose, for all that we love deeply becomes part of us.

—Helen Keller

Your Bucket List

The purpose of a bucket list is to turn some dreams into realities. Brainstorm some bucket-list activities and create a plan for how to check them off. Use the space below to create, draw, and plan. Get creative here!

Consider all the things going well in your life and what's working for you right now. Write them down. By reflecting on all the positivity you possess, you enhance your self-acceptance, self-love, and of course, hope.

A Final Word

Congratulations on completing this book! You have shown courage and vulnerability in being open with your feelings. Throughout this process, you have been asked to face the reality of your loss; begin to process big emotions; start to prepare for a life that incorporates your loss; and learn to recognize and find a new place for the memories, lessons, and love you carry as you continue your life.

You may feel differently about your loss from when you started this book, and maybe you can't describe what that difference is—that's okay. We've explored how grief isn't linear; rather, the healing process begins, stalls, and then picks up again. Give yourself permission to revisit any section of this book whenever needed. Remember, the quiet you've created through the various meditative exercises will allow you to focus on your inner thoughts and needs. What is that quiet telling you right now?

Grief and loss inevitably change us, much like any other major life event. It's a two-sided experience that often alternates between sorrow and growth. You've experienced that here through the work you did in this journal. You may have noticed that these activities, while beneficial and healthy, can be challenging for two reasons: They might remind you of other losses from your past, and sometimes we feel guilty when our mood improves from our grief work because we feel we're not honoring the loss. Ignoring grief causes it to show up in unhealthy and unproductive ways that affect us emotionally, cognitively, physically, and spiritually. Through the work you've done in this book, you've learned that pain may feel like it connects us to our loss, but there's another way to connect with our loss—a way that allows us to live our life fully while still honoring that lost part of us. Pain is merely a reminder to repeat those healing rituals and give ourselves the rest and space we need.

My wise friend Serese Brown shared with me that the grief from the death of her grandpa serves as her reminder to rest: "It always comes when I need it. It's a reminder to me of where I'm spending my time and energy. That beautiful relationship is still watching over me, knowing I need to take care of myself." I encourage you, too, to be curious about your pain, invite your grief into your space, and listen for the lessons it's trying to teach you.

Resources

Articles

American Psychological Association. naemt.org/docs/default-source
/ems-health-and-safety-documents/nemssc/ems-safety-program-guide-10-11-17.pdf.

———. apa.org/helpcenter/road-resilience.aspx.

———. "Grief: Coping with the Loss of Your Loved One." January 1, 2020. apa.org
/topics/grief.

Brody, Jane E. "Understanding Grief." *New York Times*, January 15, 2018. nytimes
.com/2018/01/15/well/live/understanding-grief.html.

Hugstad, Kristi. "Grieving Losses Other Than Death." HuffPost. July 26, 2017. huffpost
.com/entry/at-a-loss-grieving-losses-other-than-death_b_59794d8ce4b06b305561ce05.

Psychology Today. "Grief." *Psychology Today*. psychologytoday.com/us/basics/grief.

Books

Brown, Brené, PhD, LMSW. *Rising Strong: How the Ability to Reset Transforms the Way We
Live, Love, Parent, and Lead.* New York: Random House, 2017.

Edelman, Hope. *Motherless Daughters: The Legacy of Loss.* New York: Delta, 1995.

Podcasts

Forsythia, Shelby. *Coming Back: Life after Loss*. shelbyforsythia.com/coming-back-podcast# :~:text=Whether%20your%20loss%20is%20a,%2C%20divorce%2C%20illness%20and%20more.

Jeffrey, Amber. *The Grief Gang*. listennotes.com/podcasts/the-grief-gang-amber -jeffrey-4ezCcRLIYBq.

Kasemeier, Blake. *Good Grief*. listennotes.com/podcasts /good-grief-blake-kasemeier-kzMaWfdRh2E.

Provencher, Moe. *Grief/Relief*. griefreliefpodcast.com.

Stang, Heather. *The Mindfulness & Grief Podcast*. mindfulnessandgrief.com/grief-podcast/

Wellbrock, Teri. *The Healing Place*. podcasts.apple.com/us/podcast/the-healing-place-podcast /id1261995891.

TED Talks

Elmore, Shekinah. "The Courage to Live with Radical Uncertainty." ted.com/talks /shekinah_elmore_the_courage_to_live_with_radical_uncertainty.

Hone, Lucy. "Three Secrets of Resilient People." ted.com/talks/lucy_hone_3_secrets _of_resilient_people?referrer=playlist-wisdom_for_living_with_death_and_loss.

Solomon, Andrew. "How the Worst Moments in Our Lives Make Us Who We Are." ted.com /talks/andrew_solomon_how_the_worst_moments_in_our_lives_make_us_who_we_are?refer- rer=playlist-life_is_beautiful#t-73283.

Websites

The Christi Center, Austin, Texas: christicenter.org
This is a grief and loss agency that serves any child, teen, or adult who is grieving the death of a loved one. They offer all services free of charge.

GriefShare: griefshare.org
These seminars and support groups are led by people who understand what you are going through and want to help. GriefShare resources can help you recover from your loss and rebuild your life.

HealGrief: healgrief.org/grief-support-resources/
This site provides community, connections, resources, and local and national support.

Psychology Today: psychologytoday.com/us
This website has a comprehensive list of therapists within the United States. You can search by location, specialties, age, insurance, and modalities.

References

American Psychological Association. *"The Road to Resilience."* Washington, DC: American Psychological Association, 2014. Retrieved from http://www.apa.org/helpcenter /road-resilience.aspx.

Angelou, Maya. *Letter to My Daughter.* New York, NY: Random House, 2008.

Benjamin, Sonya Marie. Vessel + Spirit. Accessed February 15, 2021. http://www.vesseland spirit.com/.

Bonanno, George A. *The Other Side of Sadness: What the New Science of Bereavement Tells Us About Life After Loss.* New York, NY: Basic Books, 2010.

Bush, Ashley Davis. *Transcending Loss: Understanding the Lifelong Impact of Grief and How to Make It Meaningful.* New York, NY: William Morrow Paperbacks; 1st edition, 1994.

Chödrön, Pema. *When Things Fall Apart: Heart Advice for Difficult Times.* Boulder, CO: Shambhala, 2016.

Chopra, Deepak. *Life After Death: The Burden of Proof.* New York, NY: Random House, 2008.

Didion, Joan. *The Year of Magical Thinking.* New York, NY: Knopf Doubleday Publishing Group; Reprint edition, 2007.

Divine, Megan. *It's OK That You're Not OK: Meeting Grief and Loss in a Culture That Doesn't Understand.* Boulder, CO: Sounds True, Inc.; 1st edition, 2017.

Elle, Alexandra. *After the Rain: Gentle Reminders for Healing, Courage, and Self-Love.* San Francisco, CA: Chronicle Books, 2020.

Epstein, Mark. "The Trauma of Being Alive," *New York Times*, August 3, 2013.

Fox, Judy Z., and Mia Roldan. *Voices of Strength: Sons and Daughters of Suicide Speak Out*. Far Hills, NJ: New Horizon Press, 2008.

Fuller, Thomas. *A Pisgah-Sight of Palestine and the Confines Thereof: With the History of the Old and New Testament Acted Thereon*. London: Printed by R. Davenport for John Williams,
1662.

Hickman, Martha Whitmore. *Healing After Loss: Daily Meditations for Working Through Grief*. New York, NY:. William Morrow Paperbacks; 1st edition, 1994.

Keller, Helen. *We Bereaved* (Classic Reprint). London: Forgotten Books, 2017.

Kübler-Ross, Elisabeth. *What the Dying Have to Teach Doctors, Nurses, Clergy & Their Own Families*. New York, NY: Scribner, 2014.

Lamott, Anne. *Stitches: A Handbook on Meaning, Hope and Repair*. New York, NY: Riverhead Books; 1st edition, 2013.

Lewis, C. S. *A Grief Observed*. HarperCollins Publishers; 1st edition, 2001.

O'Neill, Stephanie. "Grief for Beginners: 5 Things to Know About Processing. *NPR, May 14, 2020*. https://www.npr.org/2020/05/12/854905033/grief-for-beginners -5-things-to-know-about-processing-loss?utm_source=npr_newsletter&utm_medium= email&utm_content=20210319&utm_term=5255231&utm_campaign=life-kit&utm _id=43906393&orgid=758&utm_att1=.

Rogers, Fred. "Fred Quotes." Fred Rogers Center for Early Learning & Children's Media. Accessed March 2, 2021. http://www.fredrogerscenter.org/about-fred/Fred-Quotes.

Strayed, Cheryl. *Wild*. New York, NY: Vintage; 1st edition, 2013.

Washam, Spring. *A Fierce Heart: Finding Strength, Courage, and Wisdom in Any Moment*. Carlsbad, CA: Hay House, Inc., 2019.

Acknowledgments

I'd like to express gratitude to Callisto Media for recognizing the need for this grief journal and collaborating with me to create such a valuable resource. I want to acknowledge the courage and dedication that is required of us all in doing work around grief and loss. I also want to recognize all of my friends, coworkers, and teachers who have shown me by example the value of generosity of spirit, kindness, and humility that have allowed me to do the work I do. Lastly, I give thanks, with all my heart, to my husband, Christopher, and our sons, Desmond and Darby, for grounding me in their love and providing me the peace, balance, and humor I need to continue to grow.

About the Author

Mia Roldan, LCSW, LCDC, is a licensed clinical social worker in Austin, Texas. Her first book, *Voices of Strength: Sons and Daughters of Suicide Speak Out*, coauthored with Judith Z. Fox, is about surviving a parent's suicide, which was Mia's personal experience. Mia utilizes the strengths perspective with all her clients to build a foundation for life that's based on self-care, community, and personal connections. Grief and loss work is something Mia has done her entire professional life with adolescents, families, and adults in different educational and medical settings. She is the clinical therapist at the Adolescent Medicine Clinic with Dell Children's Medical Group, part of the University of Texas at Austin's Dell Med Department of Health Social Work, and an assistant professor of practice at UT Austin's Steve Hicks School of Social Work. Find out more at miaroldanaustintherapy.com and uthealthaustin.org/directory/mia-roldan.

CPSIA information can be obtained
at www.ICGtesting.com
Printed in the USA
JSHW031344140921
18481JS00001BA/1